AFRICAN
renaissance

PETER MAGUBANE

AFRICAN
renaissance

text by Sandra Klopper

AMPLATS

First published in 2000 by Struik Publishers (Pty) Ltd
(a member of Struik New Holland Publishing (Pty) Ltd)

London • Cape Town • Sydney • Auckland

24 Nutford Place
London W1H 6DQ
United Kingdom

14 Aquatic Drive
Frenchs Forest
NSW 2086, Australia

80 McKenzie Street
Cape Town 8001
South Africa

218 Lake Road
Northcote, Auckland
New Zealand

Reg. no.: 54/00965/07

10 9 8 7 6 5 4 3 2 1

ISBN 1 86872 413 1

Managing editor: Annlerie van Rooyen
Designer: Janice Evans
Editor: Lesley Hay-Whitton
Proofreader: Tessa Kennedy

Reproduction by Hirt & Carter Cape (Pty) Ltd
Printed and bound by Tien Wah Press (Pte.) Ltd, Singapore

ACKNOWLEDGEMENTS
I would like to thank the following people for their help: Dr Tsiane
from Doornlaagte; Mr Tabane, Mrs Rina Chaule and Mrs Melinda
Bekker from the Basotho Cultural Village in QwaQwa National Park.
PETER MAGUBANE

FRONT COVER: A young Pedi girl; BACK COVER: South Sotho
body adornment; SPINE: A Xhosa initiate;
PAGE 1: An Ndebele wall design; PAGES 2–3: Xhosa initiates;
LEFT: A Bantwane girl; PAGES 6–7: Ndebele wall decoration.

CONTENTS

AFRICAN RENAISSANCE BY PETER MAGUBANE

In the wake of the African Century, Peter Magubane has once again brought the artful use of the lens, to ordinary South African life, whether in joy or agony, in mourning or in celebration, to the world stage. In a symphonic fashion, the power of the picture has been skilfully married to the strength of the word. More significantly, this marriage of the picture and the word, makes the book accessible to people from all walks of life, affording audiences at home and abroad, an opportunity to celebrate the African identity and heritage.

While some our customs have been forsaken, others still form an integral part of South African life, and to that extent, Magubane embeds them within a modern cultural life, to present a fascinating juxtaposition of the old and the new while at the same time preserving them for posterity.

It is also important to note that Mr Magubane is one of the best-placed persons to produce this good work. He is among the few South Africans who were able to record some of the momentous activities at the most challenging times of our history.

Seldom has a single person's talent straddled the defining epochs of our country's history from bringing the horror images of the past, to capturing the anxieties and expectations of the transition to celebrating the triumph of South Africans over adversity. Mr Magubane has, in this book, carved a way in which South Africans can enter the new millennium without forgetting who they are, where they come from and what their potential is.

Indeed, as we narrate the stories of our lives to the next generation, what will escape our frail minds, Mr Magubane's powerful images will cover. Our grandchildren will be the richer for it.

It is with all the respect to Peter Magubane's continued skills, that I proudly endorse this book.

MR JACOB ZUMA
DEPUTY PRESIDENT
REPUBLIC OF SOUTH AFRICA
May 2000

AMPLATS

Amplats is proud to sponsor *African Renaissance*, a vibrant and evocative celebration of the rich cultural heritage of the peoples of South Africa.

The brilliant photography of Peter Magubane takes us on a captivating journey through the diverse cultures of this unique and splendid land. The joy, pathos and – most of all – the pride of a nation are captured in a series of perceptive and hauntingly beautiful images.

In many respects, Amplats is a microcosm of life in South Africa, our operations a crucible of cultures that work together, as a team, towards a common goal. Since the discovery of platinum reserves in 1924, the metal has played a key role in stimulating the country's economic growth, as whole communities developed around our mines.

Demand for platinum – the metal of the future – continues to increase. It is prized as the ultimate symbol for status and elegance in jewellery, and is an integral part of many industrial and high-tech applications. As our operations grow to meet this demand, platinum is becoming increasingly important to the economic well-being of the country and the vision of the African Renaissance.

We dedicate this book to our employees, and to their contribution to making this vision a reality.

INTRODUCTION

A new era dawned for South Africa following the 1990 release from prison of Nelson Mandela and other political prisoners, the unbanning of political organisations like the African National Congress, and the return of countless South Africans who left the country in the 1960s, 70s and 80s. When the ANC assumed office after the country's first democratic election in May 1994 policies were introduced which aimed to empower marginalised and formerly disenfranchised communities. This commitment to redressing past imbalances led to the publication of the White Paper on Arts and Culture that confronted the idea of creating job opportunities in the informal sector by encouraging craft specialists, especially women from rural areas, to market their skills through newly developed channels aimed at targeting the country's burgeoning tourist industry.

ABOVE: Former President Nelson Mandela receiving royal leopard skin regalia from some of his admirers. BOTTOM, FROM LEFT TO RIGHT: Ndebele painter Francina Ndimande with her grand-child; a Tsonga woman stamping mealies; the grandmother of a Swazi bride. More often than not, older women based in rural areas play an active role in preserving and passing on indigenous cultural practices and traditions.

These attempts at validating the creative powers of those who, in many cases, produce work rooted in the experiences and values of rural traditionalists, found a powerful voice in the Africanist sentiments expressed by then Deputy President Thabo Mbeki before he assumed office as South Africa's second black leader in 1999. In 1996 Mbeki first proclaimed his vision for South Africa and Africa by asserting the importance to him of his African heritage and identity. This proud and emphatic declaration gave rise to Mbeki's concept of an African Renaissance, a cultural and economic rebirth of the country and the continent based on Africa's extraordinary history of past achievements.

Similar attempts to validate Africa's achievements by drawing attention to its remarkable past were made at various points in the course of the 20th century. For example, the 1920s Harlem Renaissance, or the 'New Negro' movement, wit-

Young children growing up in rural areas, where ritual practices form an integral part of people's daily lives, have a far better understanding of African cultural traditions than their urban counterparts.

nessed a remarkable flowering of creative energies by African American writers and artists seeking to draw inspiration from, and to celebrate, their African heritage. Nigerian leader Benjamin Azikiwe's *Renascent Africa* (1937) was another important landmark in this gradual rediscovery of a history that had been forcibly denied and therefore forgotten during the colonial period, when massive exploitation of the continent's human and natural resources went hand in hand with a refusal to honour and respect its cultural achievements. Azikiwe, who had studied in the United States of America when the Harlem Renaissance was in full swing, and who later became the Federal Republic of Nigeria's first president, refused to accept that Africa's future had been blighted forever by the impact of European imperialism. According to him, the well-being of the continent depended on reactivating a spiritual balance through respect for others; achieving social regeneration through the triumph of democracy; ensuring mental emancipation through a rejection of racism, and striving for economic prosperity through self-determination. While many other African leaders subsequently developed similar ideas in the struggle for African independence during the 1940s and 1950s, publications such as *Renascent Africa* and the Pan-Africanist writings of earlier theorists, for instance W.E.B. du Bois and Marcus Garvey, clearly paved the way for President Mbeki's integrated vision of a brave new world founded, not only on sound economic practices, but also on a profound acknowledgement of the need to preserve humanist principles.

In South Africa these principles have been passed down through deeply entrenched humanist traditions, such as the concept of *ubuntu*. This notion finds expression, most eloquently, in proverbs and sayings, among them the Sotho maxim, 'Motho ke motho ka batho' (a person is a person by people). In Zulu, this idea is voiced by the words, 'Umuntu ngumentu ngabantu', which also means that one's humanity is defined through sociability. Viewed in these terms, President Mbeki's vision of an African Renaissance is based on respect for the idea of culture as an integration between the individual and the community, as well as on an acknowledgement of the wisdom embodied in traditions that have been passed on from one generation to another as part of Africa's attempt to preserve its humanity in the face of both internal strife and external exploitation.

During the 1990s, numerous local bodies and cultural institutions embraced this challenge to build a humane and prosperous African society. Notable in this regard are the Congress of Traditional Leaders of South Africa, which emerged in the late 1980s, and the Sankofa Centre for the African Renaissance in Durban, which was launched in 1998. While the former, under the leadership of Chief Patekile Holomisa, fought to secure a place for traditional cultural practices and codes of law in South Africa's new constitution, the latter has included among its aims the validation of indigenous and contemporary African systems of knowledge, and the development of training programmes for community-based organisations. Because the concerns of the Congress of Traditional Leaders include the preservation of patriarchal values, this organisation has not always been successful in commanding respect, particularly from women, and its attempts to influence the constitutional process have proved largely unsuccessful. But it has actively endorsed the revival of various traditionalist practices in rural areas throughout South Africa.

The San today hunt and use many other skills associated with their forebears, but their ancestors are best known for the ancient rock paintings found in caves throughout southern Africa.

South Sotho male initiates
averting their gaze as
a sign of deference. This need
to show respect also explains
the fact that these initiates
often wear sunglasses at
their coming-out ceremonies.
In most communities that
still observe such rituals,
initiates receive carved staffs
as an acknowledgement of
their transition to adult status.

The growing interest, especially among rural traditionalists, in creating a cultural platform for the (re)enactment of deeply entrenched beliefs and values has led to the re-introduction of initiation ceremonies among some groups, such as the Tswana, as well as the adoption of newly invented practices among the Zulu and others. In 1995, and again in 1997, Tswana chief Sam Mankuroane organised two highly successful initiation schools. The latter was attended by over 400 girls and 2,600 boys. Since many of the initiates came from large urban centres, there can be little doubt that urban-based families also ascribe considerable importance to the impact that events of this kind are likely to have on the social, and especially moral, development of youngsters exposed to an increasingly unpredictable and often violent world. Earlier, in 1984, when Zulu king Zwelethini introduced an annual Reed Ceremony in northern KwaZulu-Natal, he found a ready audience for his project among both homestead heads, anxious to encourage young unmarried women to abandon promiscuous behaviour, and the young participants themselves, who valued the attention this event afforded them.

Despite the concerns expressed by some outside observers, who condemned the Reed Ceremony for celebrating nubility instead of fulfilling its commitment to preparing women for their future roles as mothers and homemakers, this annual event continues to enjoy the support of thousands of Zulu-speaking girls throughout KwaZulu-Natal. An attempt in 1996 to transform it into a multicultural celebration,

The 1996 Zulu Reed Ceremony was attended, not only by Zulu maidens, but also by Indian and white girls from various areas of KwaZulu-Natal. This attempt to transform the ceremony into a multicultural celebration attracted widespread interest from the general public.

largely due to King Zwelethini's growing contact at the time with leaders from the African National Congress, attracted widespread public interest. At that stage, most South Africans still expressed support for the idea of developing a 'rainbow nation', a society willing to effect a balance between promoting the interests and values of minority groups while at the same time embracing structures aimed at building a common sense of national pride. But this concept, which was first espoused by Archbishop Desmond Tutu and, later, by then President Mandela, has since been eclipsed by the notion of an African Renaissance, probably because the unashamedly Africanist focus of the latter drive effectively acknowledges the need to redress past imbalances.

Viewed from this Africanist perspective, the invitation that was extended to young Indian and, especially, white girls to attend the 1996 Reed Ceremony was probably intended to foster greater tolerance towards and understanding of previously marginalised communities. This commitment to tolerance and acceptance finds eloquent expression in a statement by a group of young Afrikaners, who voiced their optimism about South Africa's future by telling President Mbeki, 'Yesterday is a foreign country – tomorrow belongs to us!'

Like traditional leaders, organisations, such as the Sankofa Centre for the African Renaissance, have also played an important role in supporting recent initiatives to recognise the contribution to health services of traditional healers and diviners. The decision to establish a Traditional Healers' Council through the Department of Health highlights the extent to which African knowledge systems of this kind are beginning to receive official recognition. Partly through the latter initiative, the benefits of the knowledge which traditional healers have of the medicinal properties of plants are also becoming more readily available to other sectors of the population. However, the most significant indication of the growing validation that African medicinal practices have received in recent years is provided by the publication of several substantial studies aimed at recording how and why traditional healers use certain plants.

A particularly interesting issue is raised by the fact that these healers are now exploring the medicinal properties, not only of indigenous, but also of exotic plants. As this suggests, African systems of knowledge are dynamic rather than static, always ready to adapt to changing circumstances. Since rural communities often observe both indigenous and Christian rituals during various rites

RIGHT: Indigenous healers and diviners have recently been afforded official recognition by the Department of Health. BOTTOM LEFT: Bantwane women from Moutse village near Loskop Dam dressed in leather aprons and a wealth of beadwork. BOTTOM RIGHT: Zulu maidens from the Drakensberg at their coming-out ceremony, during which they receive gifts such as radios.

of passage, the same can be said of African cultural traditions. This hybrid integration of African and non-African forms and practices finds expression, most obviously, in the widespread tendency among brides to wear Western as well as indigenous forms of dress at different stages of their wedding ceremonies (see page 16). But it is also reflected in the extravagant headdresses of Durban's ricksha pullers and the richly inventive use of Christmas ornaments, plastic baby rattles and other exotic decorations by those wearing traditional forms of dress on festive and other occasions. This is not to imply that the past is no

Top: A Bantwane bride and groom arriving at their wedding dressed in Western attire.

Above: At other stages during the ceremony, the bride adopts traditional Bantwane dress.

Right: Exceptionally large clay pots are generally reserved for making beer. These Bantwane beer pots were produced in the 1920s.

longer regarded as important. Rather, it is to acknowledge that tradition is continually modified and revitalised in, and through, the present.

Notwithstanding the significance of this dynamic culture, the African Renaissance is founded on the idea of a cultural and economic rebirth based on Africa's extraordinary history of past achievements. Reflecting, in particular, on Africa's cultural heritage, President Mbeki noted in 1998, 'The beginning of our rebirth as a continent must be our own discovery of our soul, captured and made permanently available in the great works of creativity represented by the pyramids and sphinxes of Egypt, the stone buildings of Axum and the ruins of Carthage and Zimbabwe, the rock paintings of the San, the Benin bronzes and the African masks, the carvings of the Makonde and the stone sculptures of the Shona.' In South Africa, this respect for the creative skills and powers of African craftsmen and -women is revealed most obviously in the tendency among some rural communities to preserve heirlooms like clay pots, wooden meat-platters and old knobkerries, many of which are said to be infused with the spiritual powers of the ancestors, who protect the living against all forms of misfortune. But it is also evidenced in the fact that a growing number of urban dwellers have begun to express an interest in their rural roots, often adopting indigenous forms of dress on festive occasions.

For others, this interest in Africa's cultural heritage has led, not so much to attempts to renew a personal connection to long-abandoned rituals or cultural practices, but rather to a desire to preserve indigenous artefacts and various local forms of adornment and dress for future generations. Thus, although the practice of collecting items such as beadwork has long been associated either with cultural institutions like museums or with the tourist trade, beaded garments and other forms of adornment are now also being acquired by increasingly large numbers of people seeking to affirm their pride in indigenous cultural traditions. Partly because of this development, there has been a gradual awakening of interest in the aesthetic powers of rural art forms among urban communities. In contrast to earlier, newly Christianised communities who were encouraged to reject indigenous forms and practices as barbaric, contemporary South Africans from all walks of life are free to embrace their African roots, and to take from their rich cultural heritage as much (or as little) as they like. Ultimately, the renaissance of South Africa's Africanness is not only about rediscovery, but also about the reiteration of what it means to be African.

RIGHT: A married Swazi woman wearing a beaded necklace decorated with South Africa's flag.
BELOW: Contemporary forms of traditional Xhosa dress have become increasingly fashionable in recent years. Produced by designers who specialise in making clothing of this kind, it is worn to the opening of parliament, at weddings and on other ceremonial occasions.

dress & adornment

More often than not, the adoption of extravagant forms of dress and other types of adornment attests to a desire to give expression to particular social, political or religious values. In most cases specific kinds of dress or the use of various types of ornamentation are prescribed either by ritual or by conventions of respect, including deeply entrenched gender relations. Alternatively, they attest to the dictates of fashion. As such, clothing and other adornment usually underline notions of status and identity. In some situations, items of beadwork may be used to draw attention to a woman's status as the mother of an initiate who has just undergone circumcision, while in others they may play a significant symbolic role in divination practices. Traditional, as well as more contemporary, styles of dress and adornment thus provide highly visible evidence of a wide range of values and beliefs.

OPPOSITE: A married Ndebele woman wearing full ceremonial regalia, including a hat (usually associated with male dress), metal and beaded neckrings, a beaded blanket (*irari*) and a beaded veil (*umlingakobe*). In the past, Ndebele beadwork consisted mainly of white beads, but today this group wears brightly coloured beadwork similar in style to Ndebele mural paintings.

PAGES 20 AND 21: Because the head is the most conspicuous part of the body it is often afforded an important symbolic role in rites of passage. Whether it is adorned in beads, covered by a traditional head-dress or scarf, shaved or deliberately neglected, the head invariably alerts the viewer to a crucial aspect of the identity of the wearer, including age or marital status. Among young Bantwane girls from the Loskop Dam area south of Groblersdal in Mpumalanga province, initiation into adult status involves both the ritual cutting of hair and the wearing of a *sehlora*, or squirrel's tail, a round, beaded ornament that is sometimes elaborated through the addition of coins or other beadwork details. Once these Bantwane girls begin to menstruate, they are secluded for several days before participating in the *byale*, an initiation ceremony guided by the chief's principal wife. During this ritual the girl's hair is rubbed with fat and charcoal and, for the first time in her life, shaped like that of a *mosadi*, a mature or married woman (*see also* pages 22 and 23).

PAGES 22 AND 23: Only after the birth of her first child is a Bantwane woman referred to as a *mosadi*, or wife. She also begins to wear the bicycle seat headdress (*tlhotshwana*) on various ritual occasions, including all festive events such as the coming-out ceremonies of male and female initiates and weddings. Long strings of beads are attached to this headdress (OPPOSITE BOTTOM), which may also be covered with a colourful scarf. Rural Bantwane women take pride in preserving this and other forms of traditional dress linked to the celebration and, in some cases, revival of practices that have long since been abandoned by people living in large urban areas.

ABOVE AND OPPOSITE: Formerly, married women from various Zulu-speaking groups grew their hair before shaping it into either conical or bifurcated styles with the aid of mud. This structure was covered in red ochre, which is sometimes referred to as 'the blood of the earth', and which is generally believed to allude to the control a married woman's ancestors have over her fertility. Many women still grow their hair to signify their marital status to this day, but they now cover their heads with a detachable, ochre-coloured headdress (*inhloko*). Out of respect (*hlonipha*) for their husbands and their parents-in-law, these women also wear a woven fibre or beaded band (*umnqwazi*) at the base of their headdresses. In some areas, this badge of respect and the ochre-coloured headdress are adorned with elaborately styled beadwork decorations and brass studs.

PAGES 26 AND 27: Relatively few married women continue to wear traditional headdresses, but most older women of all groups now wear beautifully styled scarves as a sign of respect to the families of their husbands. These scarves are also intended to proclaim the woman's commitment to her marriage vows, playing a crucial role in communicating the sense of decorum generally regarded as appropriate in a married woman. PAGE 27, BOTTOM RIGHT: Unlike women from other areas, most Xhosa-speaking women do not buy commercially produced scarves. Instead, they decorate the coarse cotton material they use for this purpose with numerous rows of lines stitched along the four edges of the fabric.

dRESS &
African Renaissance
AdORNMENT

Opposite and Above Left: In contrast to women, men usually wear headdresses made from natural
materials such as feathers or porcupine quills and the skins of various wild animals. Today,
these may be combined with brightly coloured, commercially produced cotton fabrics, probably
because these tend to enhance the dramatic effects achieved by covering the head with furs,
feathers and quills. Above Right: Largely due to the fact that hunting has always been associated with
the male domain, it is unusual, but not unheard of, for women to wear skins and other materials
obtained from wild animals. Like the clothing and other ornaments worn throughout South Africa,
the materials employed in making headdresses thus serve to underline key aspects of the social
relations between men and women, including long-established divisions of labour.

BELOW AND OPPOSITE: Young Bantwane girls immediately prior to entering an initiation lodge prepared for them by the chief's mother. During the initiation period, they participate in a series of rituals leading to their transformation from uninitiated (*lethumasa*) to initiated (*mothepa*) girls. On occasions like these, charcoal, fat and either ash or clay are commonly used to adorn both the hair and the body. The reasons underlying the use of these materials are complex, often varying from one community to another. Generally speaking, however, adorning the head and body with clay and fat serves to draw attention to the transitional status of the initiates. This explains why all initiates wash themselves before passing to the next stage of life. In some communities, there has been a growing interest in these initiation ceremonies in recent years, which is due in part to a new-found commitment to stable values and traditions throughout post-apartheid South Africa. In 1997, for example, over 2,600 boys and 400 girls from the Groblersdal area of Mpumalanga province participated in mass initiation ceremonies of this kind.

Opposite: Among Zulu-speaking communities, the headdresses worn by married women have recently been used to express support for political figures like Chief Mangosuthu Buthelezi, the founder and leader of the Inkatha Freedom Party. Above and Top Right: Young Zulu women begin to grow their hair even before they leave their paternal homes to take up residence in the homesteads of their husbands and parents-in-law.

Right: The ochre-coloured headdresses worn by married women are decorated with beaded tapestries that draw attention either to the area from which they come, or to the religious institution to which they belong. This includes members of independent churches like the Ibandla lamaNazaretha, who wear very distinctive beadwork pieces consisting of multicoloured patterns against a white background.

LEFT AND ABOVE: Although today Ndzundza Ndebele women wear a wide variety of beaded headbands on various ceremonial occasions, there is no evidence to suggest that they did so prior to the Ndebele being forced to work as indentured labourers in the late 19th century. Their determination to retain a sense of group identity appears to have encouraged the Ndebele to develop richly inventive beadwork styles that now include the use of accessories such as old coins.

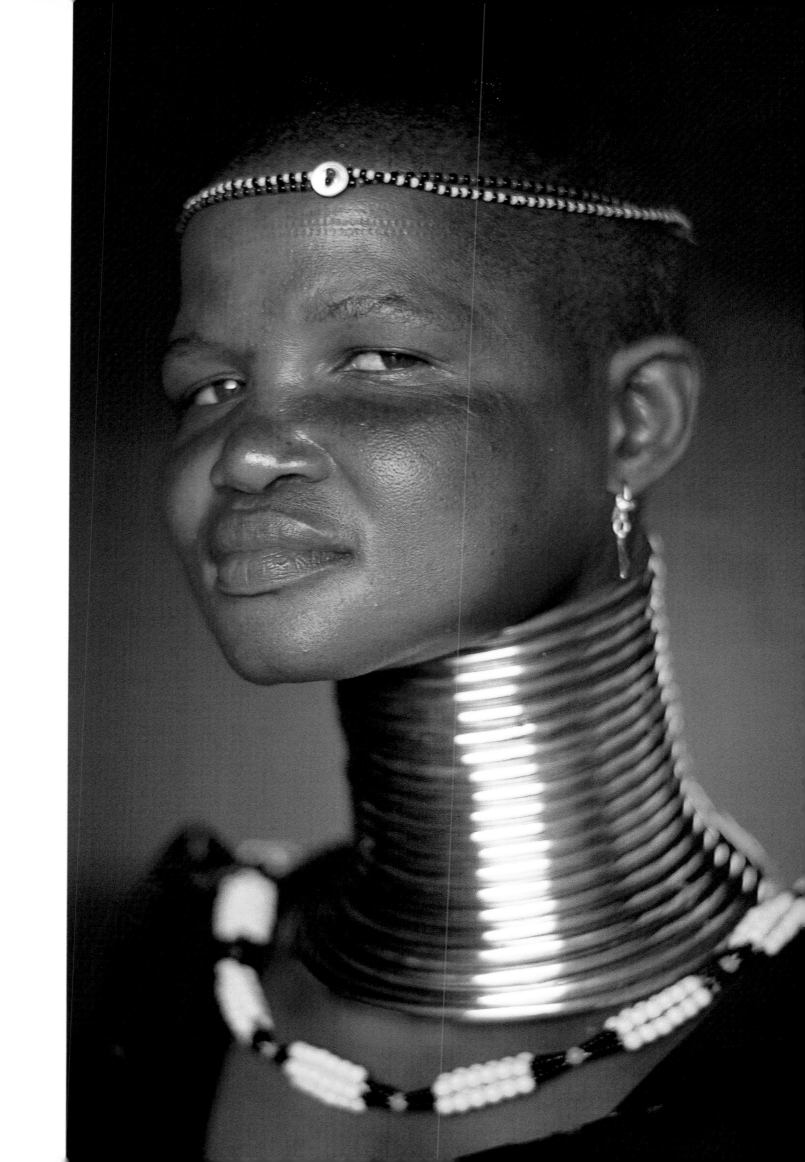

PAGES 36 AND 37: Married Ndebele women wearing permanently attached neckrings. In earlier
times, all Ndebele men provided their wives with a series of copper or brass neckrings (*iidzila*).
Mainly because these rings were regarded as a symbol of the wife's commitment to her marriage,
some women still refrain from removing them until after their husbands have died. Rings of this
kind were also considered a sign of wealth, providing visible evidence of the husband's prosperity.
OPPOSITE: The use of exceptionally wide beaded neckrings (*iirholwana*) is also common to this day,
but very few women now wear neckrings of any kind on a permanent basis. ABOVE: Instead, most
married women use clip-on metallic rings on particular ceremonial occasions.

dress & adornment

OPPOSITE AND BELOW: Bantwane women wearing beaded body and arm rings over their leather fore- and rear-aprons. These aprons (the *lebole* and the *ntepana*) are adopted only once a girl has menstruated for the first time. The practice of wearing rings around the waist, arms and neck is not restricted to the Bantwane and Ndebele (*see* page 39). Rings of this kind are also worn by Sotho groups, notably the Pedi. The adoption over a wide geographical area of similar forms of dress, including body rings and beadwork styles, attests to extensive cultural exchanges particularly in the Gauteng and Mpumalanga regions. Fostered by intermarriage and mutual participation in initiation rites, some of these cultural exchanges were first documented in the early 20th century following the decision by South Africa's then white government to curtail radically the access to land of previously independent black communities.

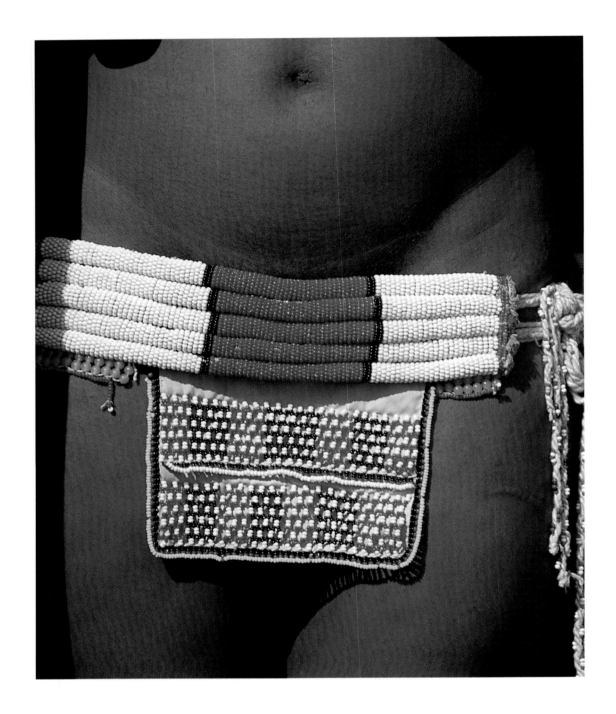

ABOVE: A young Zulu maiden wearing a beaded girdle with a small front apron. These girdles are worn on festive occasions such as the annual Reed Ceremony and Shaka Day celebrations. In the early 19th century, when beads were reserved for royalty, these girdles were made from natural fibres, usually *ubendle* leaves.

African Renaissance

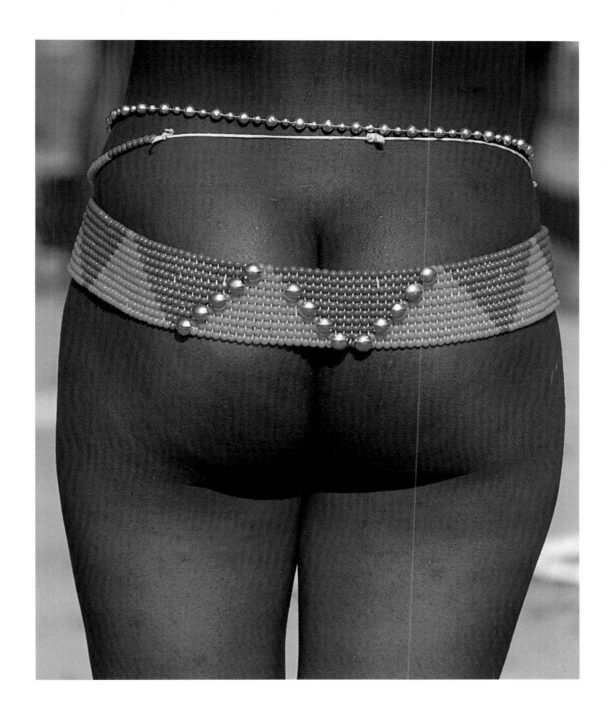

dress &

ADORNMENT

ABOVE: Once beads became freely available, numerous regional styles emerged throughout present-day KwaZulu-Natal. This explains why, to this day, the use of colour and pattern varies considerably from one area to another. Plastic beads first entered the market in the late 20th century.

43

PAGES 44 AND 45: Young Zulu women from the Drakensberg region wearing long beaded tassels probably inspired by one of the beadwork techniques more commonly used by Xhosa-speaking communities from the Eastern Cape. In contrast to the more tightly woven beadwork tapestries and other accessories worn close to the skin, these loose fronds contribute significantly to the dramatic sense of movement achieved mainly by raising one leg high above the waist during vigorous dance sequences (*see* page 120). At the coming-out ceremonies of these young women, dance sequences of this kind are interspersed with carefully choreographed displays of white and orange flags made from dusters and other cloths.

Pages 46 and 47: South Sotho initiates (*makoloana*) at their coming-out ceremonies, which are usually attended by family and friends. Initiates wear a variety of beadwork pieces generally made by their mothers, who take obvious pride in producing these gifts, which they drape over or pin onto their sons. Gifts of this kind are received shortly before each young man recites his family's ancestral praises. This recitation is believed to play a crucial role in securing the protection of one's ancestors, who ultimately ensure the fertility of all living things, and who guard their descendants against the dangers they might encounter in their daily lives.

46

At their marriage ceremonies and on other
festive occasions, Zulu men often wear
old waistcoats covered in beadwork panels.
PAGE 48, TOP RIGHT: Those made by women of
the *Ibandla lamaNazaretha* (*see* page 33)
usually incorporate brightly coloured beads
more commonly associated with beadwork
produced for the fashion industry. PAGE 48, TOP
LEFT, AND BOTTOM LEFT AND RIGHT; AND PAGE 49:
The beadwork from the Ceza-Nongoma district
in northern KwaZulu-Natal is made from more
traditional colours. This beadwork style is further
distinguished by the fact that it consists of
intricately conceived geometric patterns, shaped
from variously coloured squares and triangles.

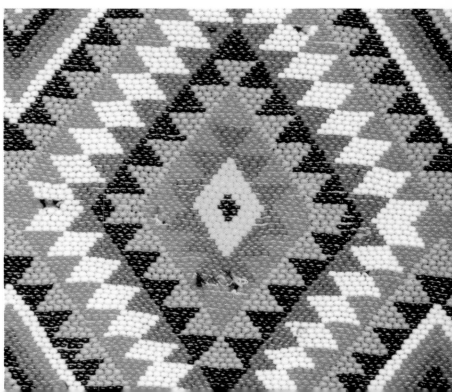

ABOVE: Married Zulu women commonly wear capes as a sign of respect. In the lower Drakensberg,

capes (*izibheklane*) are decorated with long, narrow beadwork panels sewn onto layers of cloth.

The varied designs found on these panels attest to the remarkable creativity in this region.

ABOVE: Near Durban, in the Valley of a Thousand Hills, the capes worn by married women generally consist almost entirely of large plastic beads. Unusual optical effects are created by interspersing black beads with multicoloured ones and through the use of safety pins as decorative motifs.

dRESS &
African Renaissance
AdORNMENT

OPPOSITE AND BELOW: On festive occasions Swazi men (and women) wear necklaces consisting of two small beadwork panels. More often than not, these panels are today decorated with distinctive, non-traditional designs like the South African flag (see page 17) and the letters SD, a reference to the number plates found on Swaziland's cars. Older, married men also wear leopard skin headbands (OPPOSITE) as an indication of their status and their authority over younger members of their families.

ABOVE: Throughout South Africa, diviners continue to act as intermediaries between the living and the dead. In some cases, they do so by interpreting the needs of the ancestors, which are revealed in the seemingly random configurations of bones and shells which they scatter on the ground in response to their clients' queries. OPPOSITE: These diviners wear highly distinctive beadwork styles and colours, generally favouring black, white and red beads.

The diviner (*isangoma*), who can be either male (OPPOSITE) or female (ABOVE), always carries a
number of accessories, including a switch (*ishoba lengoma*) made from tail hairs of a ritually
slaughtered ox. These switches are usually white, the colour of the ancestors. In some situations,
the diviner's switch may be used for sprinkling medicines, but its ritual importance is underlined,
above all, by the fact that it plays a crucial role in the coming-out ceremonies of novice diviners.
OPPOSITE: All diviners wear gall bladders obtained from ritually slaughtered animals at certain times.
These bladders protect their mediating powers, enabling them to interpret the needs of the dead,
who can and do cause illness among the living if they are not remembered and appeased.

PAGES 58 AND 59: The use of plastic beads has become increasingly common throughout South Africa, which can be ascribed partly to the fact that it is much quicker to produce beaded garments sewn from these large beads. Other factors such as the cost of smaller glass beads also help to account for this development. In the past, outsiders buying beadwork items from rural communities generally avoided acquiring garments sewn from these plastic beads, but private collectors and museums now realise that the use of plastic beads has led to the development of new aesthetic concerns. It has encouraged the production of unusually boldly patterned beadwork pieces and an interest in increasingly synthetic colour combinations. Plastic beads are now worn in a variety of different contexts, both by initiates (LEFT, AND OPPOSITE LEFT AND RIGHT) and by older women (see page 51) and men.

PAGES 60 AND 61: Historically, metal bangles made from imported brass or copper wire were regarded as symbols of wealth and status. Once this trade item became freely available, the practice of wearing metal ornaments spread rapidly throughout southern Africa. Although today many women still wear bangles, they are now made from tin alloys and other comparatively inexpensive metals.

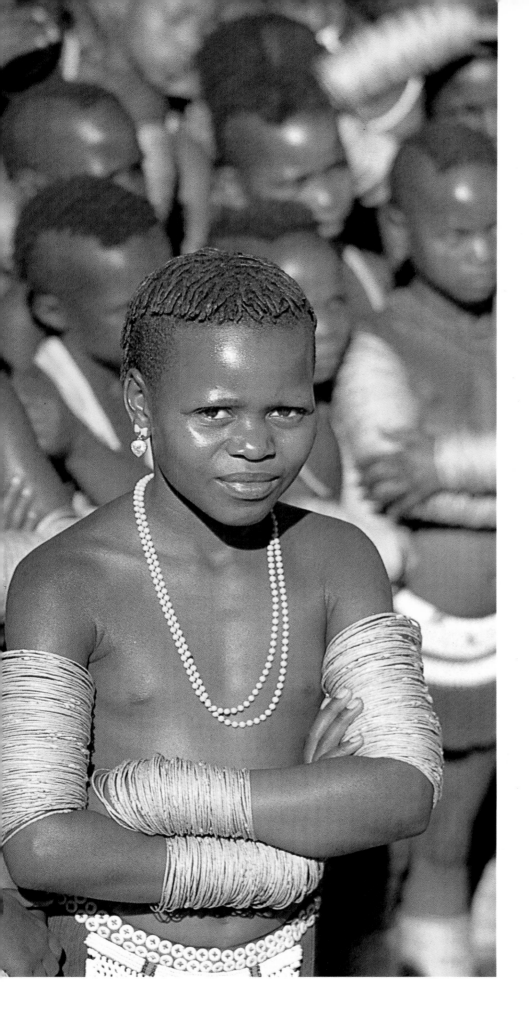

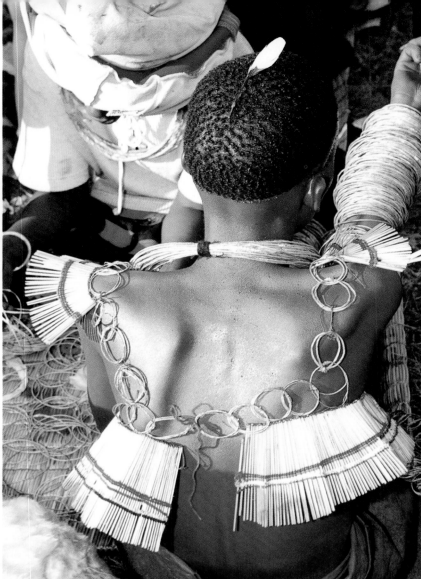

Like initiates in many other parts of Africa, Bantwane girls from the Groblersdal area of
Mpumalanga province (PAGES 62 AND 63) and Pedi girls from the Ga-Mphahlele area (PAGES 64
AND 65) discard their normal, everyday clothing before they enter the initiation lodge.
The adoption during their seclusion of grass garments and ornaments is usually informed by
important symbolic considerations. Because grass is an ephemeral material, it obviously draws
attention to the fact that initiation is a temporary condition. More importantly, though, the grass
garments worn by these initiates allude to the idea of growth and fertility and hence also to the
fact that girls' initiation ceremonies mark the onset of menstruation. In other words, initiation
ceremonies of this kind ultimately celebrate the fact that women bear children. During their
confinement in these initiation lodges girls receive instruction in appropriate social and
sexual behaviour aimed at preparing them for their future roles as wives and mothers.
OPPOSITE: In some situations, young initiates are rewarded with sweets strung into long
garlands when they emerge from the initiation lodge.

DRESS &
ADORNMENT

OPPOSITE AND BELOW: It is quite common for people like these Ndebele women to wear traditional forms of dress in combination with fashion accessories, such as peaked caps, berets, and sunglasses. These hybrid dress styles have become so entrenched that they now play an integral role in giving expression to important aspects of the wearer's identity. Among the Ndebele, for example, hats, caps and berets are considered essential accessories for married women, fulfilling much the same role as scarves or more traditional headdresses among other southern African communities (*see* pages 26–27). In contrast to berets and scarves, the use of sunglasses is not gender-specific. Because of the harsh weather conditions encountered in South Africa's summers, they obviously fulfil a purely practical role in protecting people against the sun's glare. They are often adopted by initiates emerging from a period of seclusion, who wear them as a sign of deference but generally also associate them with the worldly sophistication of adult life.

PAGES 68 AND 69: Many of the accessories adopted by the Bantwane on festive occasions, such as weddings, were originally intended for other purposes: Christmas decorations are transformed into sparkling necklaces, while pot lids may be used as percussion instruments.

PAGES 70 AND 71: Young South Sotho women often carry ribbons from flower bouquets and plastic baby rattles at their coming-out ceremonies, when they are known as *ditswejane*. In recent years, the recycling of commercial goods has become increasingly common.

ABOVE: Although dwarfed by the bulbous legrings which young Ndebele women wear on festive

occasions, their tennis shoes or tackies have become an obligatory part of their traditional

costumes. OPPOSITE: Other accessories, like mirrors, are also commonly worn by people of all ages.

Used as neck ornaments, these mirrors often create blinding reflections in the midday sun, but

when they are worn near a fire after dark they tend to cast strange, smoky lights into the night.

Until the late 18th century when imported cloth was introduced into southern Africa by English and

Portuguese traders, local communities made clothing from tanned leather. PAGES 74 AND 75: By the

late 19th century, the use of cotton had become so widespread that it began to play an integral

role in various forms of traditional dress throughout the region. PAGE 76, LEFT: Today, married Tsonga

women from the Lowveld region near the Kruger National Park tie chiffon or cotton cloths (*minceka*)

over their billowing skirts. PAGE 76, RIGHT: The custom of decorating cotton cloths with safety pins

has also become increasingly common in various regions. PAGE 77, LEFT: Among Xhosa communities living in the Eastern Cape, the practice of sewing black ribbon tape and pearl buttons onto white or ochre-coloured cotton was first introduced in the course of the 19th century. PAGE 77, RIGHT, AND PAGE 74, BOTTOM: The commemorative cloths worn mainly by Swazi men and women first became available a few decades ago. These ready-to-wear cotton rectangles are now so popular that they have come to fulfil important symbolic functions formerly reserved for leather garments.

ABOVE LEFT AND RIGHT: The Tsonga practice of decorating *minceka* with bold designs has
increased rapidly in recent years mainly because the development of embroidery skills has
been encouraged by self-help workshops seeking to market hand-embroidered cloths, tapestries
and cushion covers produced in rural areas. OPPOSITE: South Sotho women have developed a
highly distinctive style by sewing brightly coloured ribbon tape onto their cotton dresses.

PAGES 80 AND 81: South Sotho initiates (*makoloana*) at their coming-out ceremony waiting to be released by the master of the initiation lodge. On these occasions, young men are laden with gifts, including strings of beads, scarves and handkerchiefs (*see also* page 75 bottom). The boldly patterned and coloured cloths pinned to the blankets that initiates wear on these occasions serve to celebrate their return to normal life where they are now expected to assume such adult responsibilities as work and marriage.

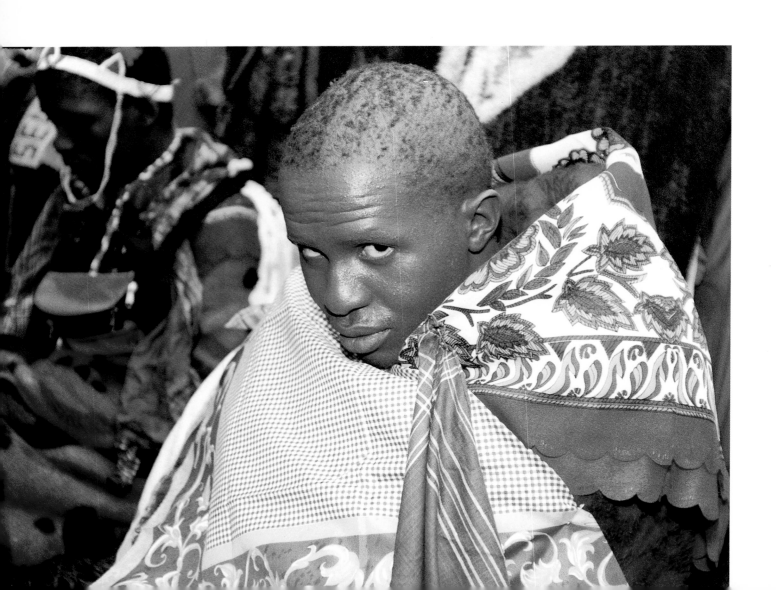

PAGES 82 AND 83: Ndebele women and Ndebele initiates (*amasokane*) commonly wear red, blue and yellow 'Middelburg' blankets that echo the bright colours found on the murals and in the beadwork associated with this group. These blankets obviously fulfil important practical functions, but over the years they have also become increasingly important markers of Ndebele identity. Like the leather karosses (*linaga*) formerly worn by this group, blankets (*irari*) traditionally have oblong beaded panels sewn onto them at regular intervals. Because the sale of these blankets to outside collectors has become increasingly lucrative since the late 1970s, few Ndebele themselves still own beaded blankets, or make beadwork panels of this kind for their own use.

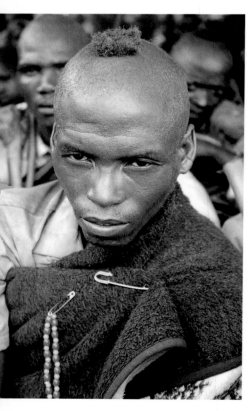

Among most southern African communities that still practise initiation and circumcision rites, like the Pedi (Above), the Tswana (Left, Opposite, Page 86, and Page 87, Top), and the Ndebele (Page 87, Bottom), young men discard their everyday clothes in favour of blankets when they enter the initiation lodge. The wearing of these blankets underlines both their willingness to leave their former lives behind them and their transitional status during the initiation period. Different coloured and patterned blankets are worn by initiates from different regions. In contrast to the 'Middelburg' blankets used by Ndebele initiates, those worn by the Bantwane and Pedi are comparatively dark, while blankets used by South Sotho initiates vary considerably both in colour and pattern. Since this can also be said of the beadwork pieces these South Sotho initiates receive on their return from the initiation lodge (*lebollo*), there can be little doubt that complex historical processes have contributed to the different ways in which southern African communities give visible expression to their sense of group identity.

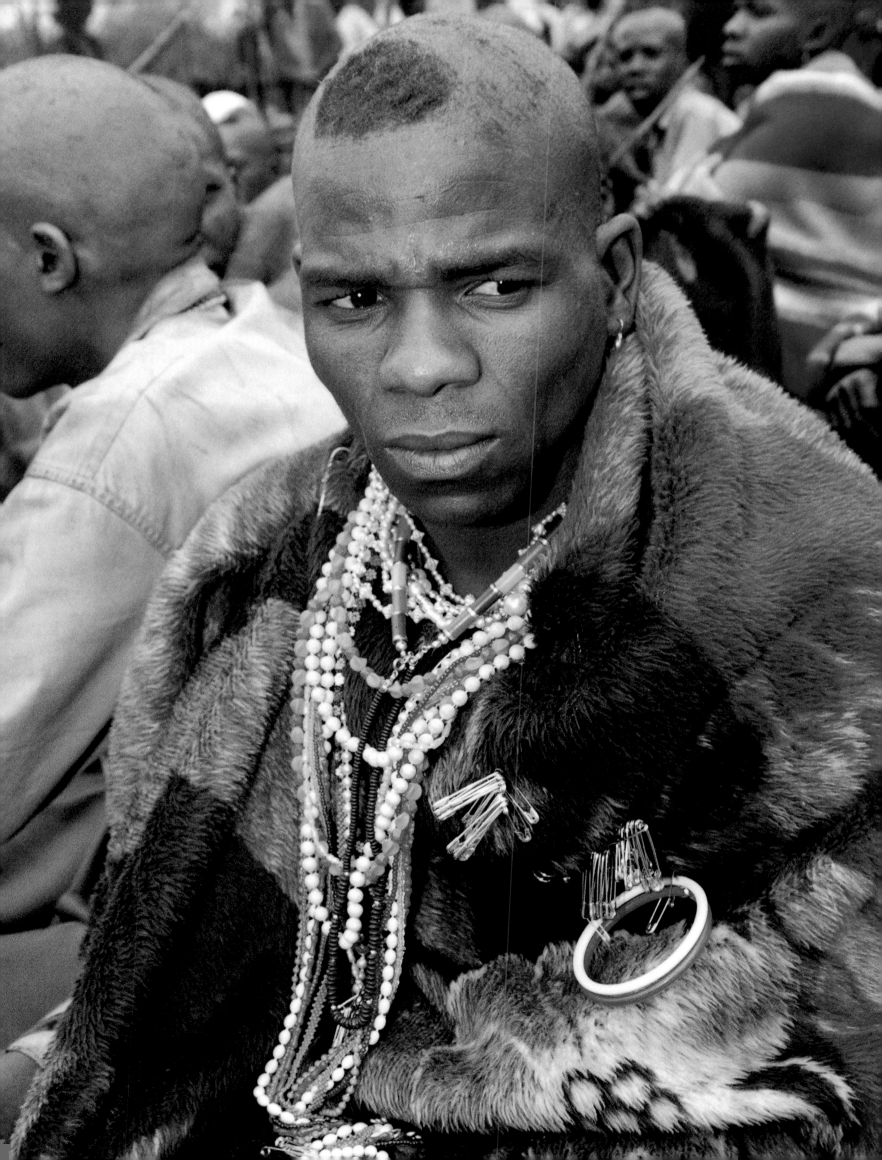

Above and Opposite: Before initiation Xhosa boys are referred to as *amakhwenkwe*. During the initiation period, when they are known as *abakwetha*, most young men wear red and white blankets to symbolise the presence of the ancestors who take care of all initiates while they are away from their homes. Below: While the initiation lodge and the blankets they wore during their seclusion are being burnt, Xhosa initiates, now known as *amakrwana*, acknowledge their future commitment to adult responsibilities by walking away from the past without ever looking back.

RiTES of PASSAGE

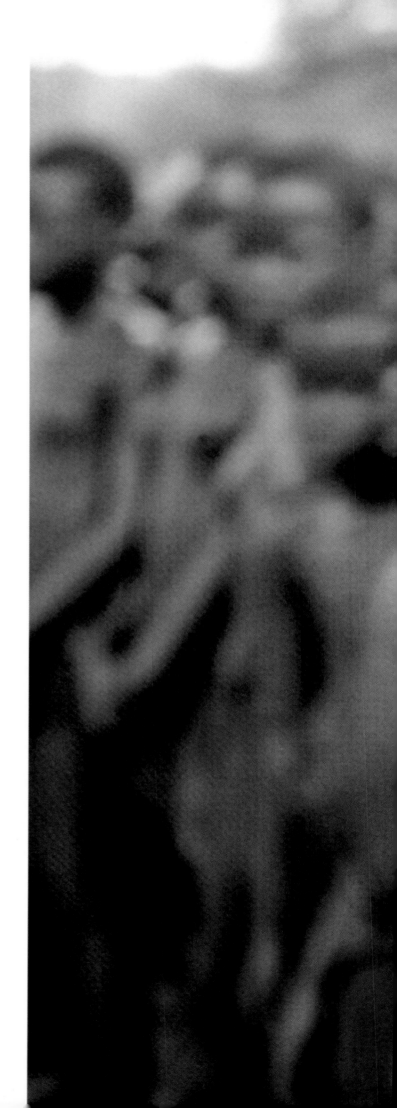

Throughout southern Africa, all of the major transitions in life are marked by appropriate celebrations or ceremonies. From birth to death, these rites of passage regulate and give expression to meaningful transitions in people's lives. Although it is only in some communities that the transformation of boys and girls into young or potential adults is marked by rites of puberty or circumcision, the transition to married life is always accompanied by rituals aimed at highlighting the new roles that men, and especially women, must assume once they begin to live together.

RIGHT: A young Pedi girl covered in *letsoku,* a mixture of red clay and fat worn by all initiates.

RiTES of
African Renaissance
PASSAGE

Until the late 18th century all chiefdoms in southern Africa observed various initiation practices to prepare young men and women for their future roles in adult society. In present-day KwaZulu-Natal, however, these rites were abandoned in favour of age-grade regiments more than a generation before the rise to power, in the early 19th century, of the first Zulu king, Shaka. Among some groups, like the Pedi, male and female initiation rites tend to coincide with the transition to puberty, but among others, like the Xhosa and Ndebele, male circumcision practices are delayed until men are in their late teens or early twenties. Female initiation rites sometimes include mock circumcision, as among the Bantwane, but, because these ceremonies are generally intended to prepare young women for their roles as wives and mothers, they usually focus on underlining appropriate social and sexual practices.

BELOW AND OPPOSITE: Pedi girls from the Ga-Mphahlele area wearing the short, stringed front apron (*lebole* or *theto*) and leather back apron (*nthepana*) adopted on these occasions.

PAGES 94 AND 95: While male initiation rites are invariably marked by circumcision, girls' initiation ceremonies do not involve any form of mutilation. The latter are nevertheless accompanied by important rituals. Among the Venda, for example, girls formerly attended three initiation schools: *vhusha*, at puberty, *tshikanda*, an intermediary school, and *dombani*, a pre-marital school which is still held to this day in some areas (PAGE 94, TOP). The *dombani* is characterised by a dance (*domba*) symbolizing the movement of a python which Venda traditionalists associate with fertility. While Venda female initiation practices have become comparatively unusual in recent years, ceremonies of this kind have been revived by groups like the Tswana (PAGE 95, BOTTOM), and the Bantwane, usually in an attempt to stamp out what some traditionalists regard as declining moral values.

PAGES 96 AND 97: The temporary dwellings Xhosa initiates (*abakwetha*) occupy after circumcision are made from ephemeral materials such as old sacking, grass and cardboard boxes strung over a precarious framework of sticks and poles. In urban areas like Cape Town, where initiation lodges are sometimes set up in fields along the N2 motorway, these dwellings tend to be covered in black refuse bags. Some initiates also use cardboard boxes to make temporary hats which they often adorn with feathers and other objects collected in the vicinity of their bush shelters.

PAGES 98 AND 99: Although masking practices, like those found among South Sotho groups living in Lesotho and the Free State, are comparatively rare in the southern African region, the use of masks is commonly associated with initiation rites elsewhere in Africa. In most cases these initiation masks, which are made from ephemeral materials by the initiates (*bale*) themselves, are burnt once the initiation period has been concluded. Like the grass belts (*likholokoane*) worn by these initiates, their grass masks celebrate the idea of (female) fertility. It is also important to note, however, that women traditionally make household items like grass mats and baskets. By learning to make initiation masks young girls are therefore introduced to one of the adult skills they may be required to use in later life.

98

The transformation of the head and face associated with initiation rites can take several different forms. ABOVE: Among South Sotho groups living in Lesotho and the Free State, female initiates (*bale*) paint their faces with Vaseline mixed with red and yellow ochre at their coming-out ceremonies. OPPOSITE, AND PAGES 102 AND 103: During initiation, Xhosa initiates rub their faces and bodies with white clay (*ifutha*) to signify the protection which their ancestors afford them during this crucial transition from childhood to adult life. This clay is washed off at the end of the initiation period before they smear themselves with fat or butter.

ABOVE AND OPPOSITE: Most of the ancestors, whose presence is signified by the white clay (*ifutha*)
and blankets worn by Xhosa initiates (*abakwetha*), are deceased senior males of the agnatic
group, but all those who die can become ancestral spirits capable of influencing the lives of
their descendants. Once an initiate has emerged into adult life, he must begin to play an active
role in preserving the well-being of his family by officiating at periodic ritual slaughterings,
usually of goats, organised in honour of the deceased, who brood over the eaves and thresholds
of their descendants' homesteads. All initiates must therefore learn to heed the wishes of the
ancestors, who communicate with their descendants through diviners, dreams and omens.
PAGES 106 AND 107: South Sotho female initiates also paint clay onto their bodies; some of these
decorations (PAGE 107) are similar to the flower and other motifs married women paint on their
houses. In this way, these patterns may be said to allude to the future life of the initiate.

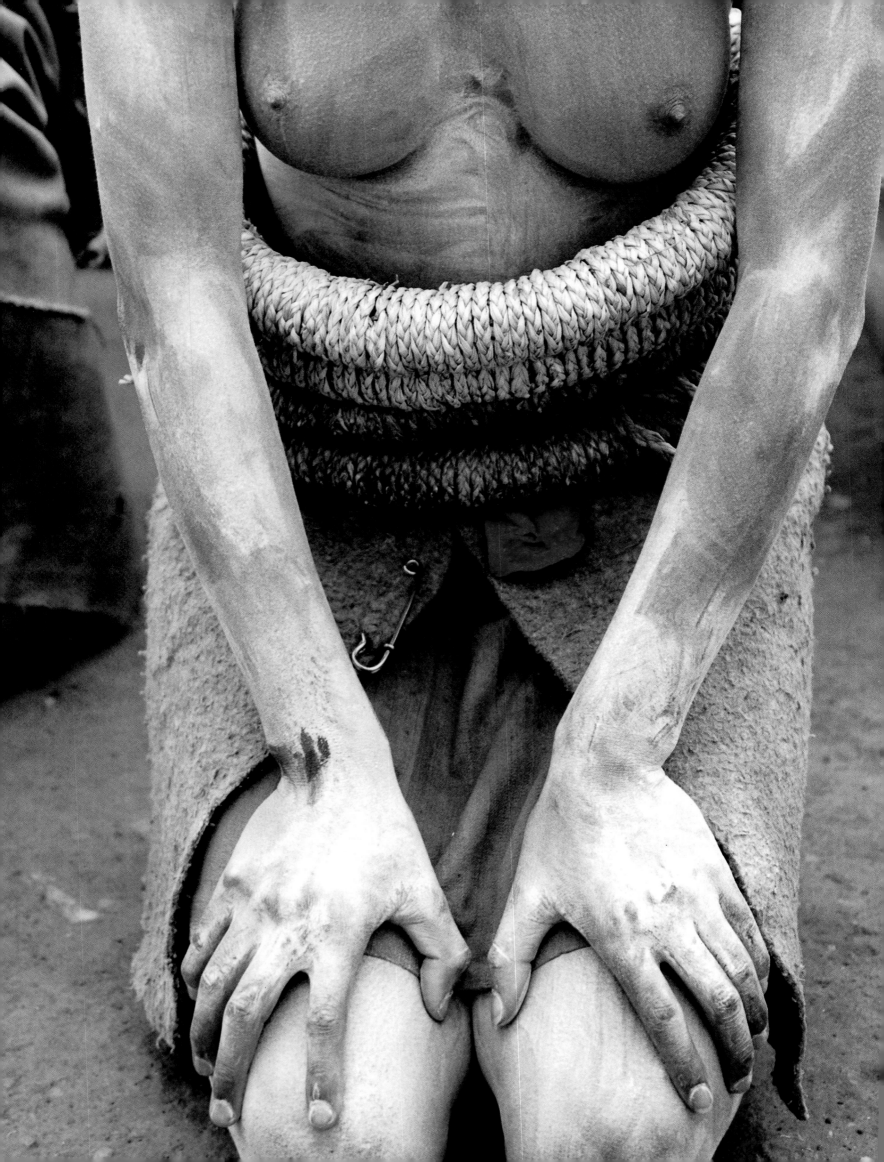

PAGES 108 AND 109: Male initiates typically receive a stick or knobkerrie at coming-out ceremonies as a symbol of their new-found status as men. The heads of many knobkerries given to Ndebele initiates (PAGE 108, BOTTOM) are fashioned from the bulbous roots of certain trees. In some rural areas knobkerries of this kind continue to be used for defensive purposes or to hunt small game. Among the South Sotho and Xhosa, the initiation period is used to perfect the stick fighting skills of young men. This martial art is also taught at some schools in KwaZulu-Natal. It has become increasingly common to obtain these sticks from curio outlets supplying the tourist market with walking sticks made from indigenous hardwoods (PAGE 109, TOP), but some are still made by specialist carvers.

The styles of sticks vary from one area to another. Bantwane (Right) and South Sotho initiates (Opposite, Bottom Left) carry knobkerries with comparatively short shafts. In the past, these sticks were frequently decorated with geometric designs woven from brass or copper wire, but many now have designs fashioned either from multicoloured plastic-coated copper wire or beads. Opposite, Bottom Right: Tswana initiates' sticks are often surmounted by crudely carved human heads. Opposite, Top: Among the Swazi, where the practice of carrying sticks on other festive occasions like weddings remains quite common, vague allusions to the human head were recorded as early as the late 19th century.

PAGES 112 AND 113: Swazi traditional
healers at their coming-out ceremony.
On these occasions, every novice
healer (*isangoma*) is anointed with
the blood of ritually slaughtered
goats. Initiates also emulate the
movements of animals eating at a
trough and demonstrate their skills in
communicating with the ancestors
before they are allowed to graduate.
In some communities, most of these
healers are female, but it is not unusual
for men to heed a calling by the
ancestors to serve people in this way.

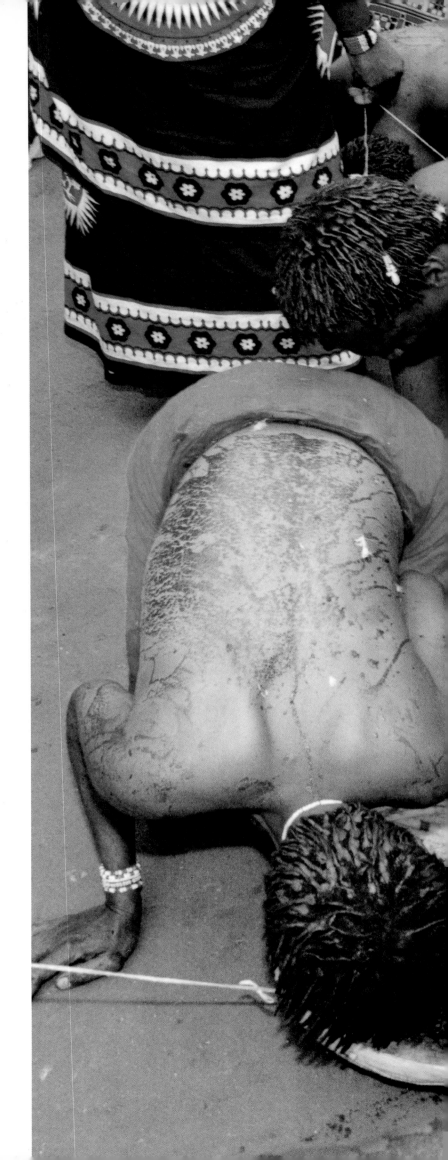

Rural weddings among the Swazi (LEFT AND OPPOSITE, TOP) and Zulu (OPPOSITE, BOTTOM) are characterised by a number of similar traditions. These include the practice of giving the bride a knife; historically she would use this knife to pierce the stomach of a ritually significant beast near the gall area. According to some traditionalists, the piercing of this animal symbolises the bride's loss of virginity. LEFT: Once the beast has been slaughtered, the gall is poured over the bride's feet before the gall bladders themselves are tied to her head. The bladders signify the presence and therefore the blessing and acceptance of the bride by the groom's ancestors. Because of the importance ascribed to the ancestors in these marriage rites, their praises are always sung during the ritual slaughtering of the beast, which takes place in the cattle byre of the groom's family.

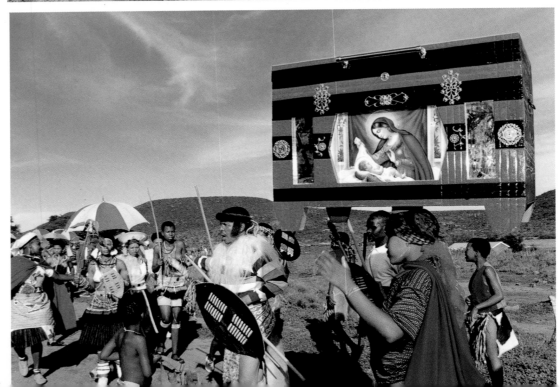

PAGES 116 AND 117: At an *umshado*, a Zulu wedding (OPPOSITE AND RIGHT), and an *umthimba*, a Swazi wedding (ABOVE), the bride's family arrive with household gifts for the bridal couple and the groom's family. In KwaZulu-Natal, this may include money pinned to the bride's head-dress (RIGHT) and kists decorated with Christian icons (OPPOSITE). These hark back to the European practice of giving brides kists containing clothes and linen, but it is not clear how this tradition was introduced into late 20th-century KwaZulu-Natal. Wedding gifts from the bride's family are off-set by *ilobolo* paid to her father by the groom. Traditionally such payments were made in cattle but, because of inadequate access to grazing and other changes in the domestic economy of rural families, they now include cash payments, bicycles, and clay and iron pots.

117

PAGES 118 AND 119: Among groups like the Tswana there has been a revival of traditional forms of dress at weddings and other ceremones. As a result, some bridal parties appear in leather karosses similar to those used in the 19th century, when imported cotton cloth was not yet freely available. Chief Sam Mankuroane with his wife and attendants (ABOVE) wearing leopard skin regalia at his 1999 wedding. The association of leopard skin with chiefly authority has a long history throughout Africa.

In keeping with this emphasis on traditionalism, guests often participate in practices that are becoming obsolete in many areas, such as demonstrations of horse-riding and dancing (OPPOSITE).

Throughout southern Africa, the celebration of rites of passage like Swazi weddings (OPPOSITE) and Zulu coming-out ceremonies (RIGHT) is often centred around competitive displays of dancing. Dancers demonstrating their skills on these occasions are encouraged by onlookers, who generally provide the necessary musical accompaniment. ABOVE: In the early 20th century, Tsonga and other men working on South Africa's mines performed these celebratory displays of dancing for the entertainment of white officials and, later, large numbers of tourists. The competitions organised by these teams of dancers echo those associated with rural weddings, where guests of the bride and bridegroom often indulge in competitive displays of skill.

PAGES 122 AND 123: Drums play a crucial role in various rituals, including religious ceremonies, weddings and initiation rites. OPPOSITE, TOP: Among some groups, notably members of independent churches like the *Ibandla lamaNazaretha*, these drums are similar to those first introduced to South Africa by British military bands. ABOVE: Other drums are based on the African model of stretching a skin membrane over only one end of a hollow wooden vessel.

Bugles are still made from the horns of various animals (Pages 124 and 125), but cheap plastic whistles (Pages 126 and 127) have replaced those formerly made from indigenous materials, such as split quills. Women are the chief performers of bugles and whistles at weddings and other important ceremonies; generally speaking, older women play the bugle, while younger women blow whistles to punctuate both their own, and other people's, dance sequences at appropriate intervals. Whistling pitch and rhythm vary considerably from one context to another. In some cases, young women perform in unison, interspersing their dances with the piercing sounds that emanate from the colourful plastic whistles that remain in their mouths throughout these performances.

ARTS & CRAFTS

There is an exceptionally vibrant artistic tradition throughout South Africa. Many aspects of this tradition date back to pre-colonial times when carved household goods, clay pots, grass baskets and gourd vessels were produced and used on a daily basis. In the course of the 20th century, new practices also emerged, including the production of large clay sculptures and murals painted with the aid of commercially produced paints. These and older crafts now tend to be dominated by women, mainly due to the need to generate income in outlying rural areas, where many of them still continue to live, raising children and engaging in subsistence farming while their husbands work in large urban centres. Through the intervention of self-help groups, certain crafts have been developed specifically for the tourist market since the mid-20th century; but, because clay pots and other household items are made both for this market and for domestic use, local artistic traditions have repeatedly been revitalised through the impact on producers of different consumer groups with sometimes vastly incompatible needs.

OPPOSITE: A woman from KwaZulu-Natal making
a basket for sale to the tourist market.

ABOVE AND OPPOSITE: The production in northern KwaZulu-Natal of colourful grass baskets is rooted in the male practice of making woven lids (*izimbenge*) for clay beer pots. However, the present tradition of weaving baskets for sale to exclusive craft shops also owes much to the active role of Swedish missionaries in developing possibilities for income generation among women living in outlying rural areas such as Hlabisa, especially in the 1970s. Since a single basket can take several weeks to complete, most women devote long hours to weaving these baskets after tending to their fields and vegetable gardens in the early mornings.

PAGES 132 AND 133: The production of clay pots by specialist female potters is still very common
throughout South Africa. Some of these pots, like those produced by the Nala family in the
Kranskop district of KwaZulu-Natal (ABOVE LEFT), have won prizes at international craft fairs and
are now made mainly for sale to outside buyers. Likewise, commercially produced pots, painted
with designs similar to those found on the wall of Ndebele homesteads (BELOW RIGHT), have
become extremely popular among middle class urban consumers in Johannesburg and elsewhere.
Clay pots are still produced for local consumption, however (ABOVE RIGHT, BELOW LEFT, and OPPOSITE).
While these may be used for a variety of different functions, they are associated most commonly
with the drinking of home-brewed beer on important festive occasions dedicated to honouring
and remembering the ancestors. The beer for these occasions continues to be served in clay
pots, partly because it is believed that the ancestors might have difficulty recognising
unfamiliarly shaped, commercially made containers.

ABOVE AND OPPOSITE: In outlying rural areas it is always women who take responsibility for the production of beer strainers and pots, as well as the decoration of walls and gourds. Many of these crafts are practised by specialists, who produce various items for sale to other members of their communities. Thus women generally rely on skilled potters and other craft specialists to supply their needs; but many also learn to decorate walls at an early age, usually by watching or helping their mothers to restore or renew these mural decorations. Because murals of this kind are painted on clay walls, they tend to deteriorate very quickly. Women living in rural areas where this art is still practised are consequently encouraged to develop and perfect their skills in making complex geometric designs throughout their adult lives.

PAGES 136 AND 137: Some Ndebele muralists, like Esther Mahlangu (OPPOSITE, TOP), have attained international fame, participating in major shows, for instance *Magicians of the Earth* held in Paris in 1989. This fame has generated important commissions, including ones from BMW, which pays internationally acclaimed artists to paint cars, and British Airways, which has adopted the practice of employing artists to design works for the tails of their aeroplanes. To accommodate the growing need of this new market, Ndebele muralists like Mahlangu (and her young pupils) have taken to producing mural designs on surfaces such as paper and canvas that can be transported and sold all over the world.

PAGES 138 AND 139: The custom of covering vessels and sticks with carefully woven decorations made from plastic-coated copper wire originally intended for electrical purposes has a long and interesting history. Although today weaving is generally associated with women, largely because of the intervention of missionaries, this art was dominated by men in several 19th-century southern African communities. There is a clear historical link between weaving and wirework, which helps to explain why this art is still commonly practised by men, some of whom decorate sticks, cover bottles with wirework designs and make wirework containers in various shapes and sizes. This use of wirework can be traced back to the making of beer pot lids (*izimbenge*) by migrant labourers working as night watchmen in urban centres like Johannesburg and Durban. Unable to obtain the grasses normally used in the production of these lids, some watchmen began making *izimbenge* from plastic-coated copper wire.

Pages 140 and 141: Among some groups like the Venda, the proliferation of sculptural traditions in the late 20th century can be linked to the production of didactic figures for use in initiation contexts, notably the *dombani*. Today, there is little if any relationship between the themes explored in these initiation figures and the works produced by contemporary sculptors for sale in exclusive galleries. However, since many of these recent works are inspired by local myths and folktales, they remain rooted in African values and traditions.

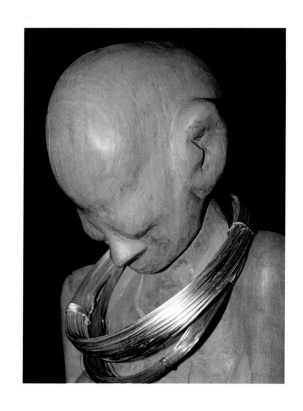

PAGES 142 AND 143: In keeping with the fact that women historically worked in clay while men produced household and other carved items from wood, the sculptor Noria Mabasa (BOTTOM LEFT) began her career in the 1970s by making pottery vessels and clay figures. Partly as a result of the acclaim she received for her works after exhibiting in urban centres and abroad from the mid-1980s onwards, Mabasa soon expanded both her repertoire and her use of materials, increasingly working in wood, producing images suggested by the shapes of branches and roots. Unlike her clay figures, these carvings (see page 141, bottom left) can be transported without breaking in transit.

Pages 144 and 145: The production of clay figures for use in initiation contexts and as fertility dolls has been documented among several southern African communities. Historically, clay was also used by boys to make toy oxen and other animals. Although it is possible that the large clay sculptures placed by the Ndebele at the entrance to homesteads (Above and Opposite) may have been inspired by these traditions, it is more likely that they are rooted in Western practices. In keeping with Western tradition, more especially public sculptures, many of these Ndebele figures are placed on raised plinths. Most of them also seem either to emulate the gestures associated with representations of important politicians, or to recreate the practice of depicting seated figures of older men. As such, many are probably intended to caricature white farmers and politicians.

HOMESTEADS

Women throughout southern Africa continue to decorate their homes with bold geometric designs using either indigenous clays or commercially available paints. Because most of these murals appear on the walls of courtyards and the exterior walls of houses and rondavels, they are clearly produced for public consumption. Enjoyed and admired by others in the community, they provide an important outlet for the expression of female creativity. In some areas, new designs are painted on the walls of dwellings and courtyards every year after the summer rains.

LEFT: The designs found on Tsonga homesteads are produced from a variety of clays to create a rich geometric patchwork of autumn colours.

147

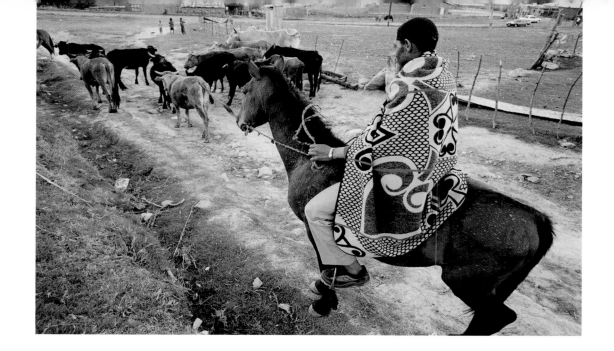

Pages 148–9, and Opposite: Tswana and South Sotho communities decorate their homes in a variety of geometric and organic designs. Known as *litema* among the South Sotho, some of these designs consist simply of lines engraved in the wet mud surface of newly prepared walls, while others are brightly coloured. Many of the motifs found on these houses are also used to frame doors and windows. More often than not, these frames are further accentuated through the use of raised mud surrounds. The patterns adorning these homes are generally derived from floral designs that evoke nature's fecundity. Above: Several of these natural motifs appear to have been inspired by patterns found on the blankets commonly worn by rural traditionalists, many of whom still ride ponies. Below: They also continue to build stone enclosures for their animals, mainly to protect sheep and young calves from small predators like jackals and wild cats.

PAGES 152 AND 153: The Ndzundza Ndebele started producing their bold mural designs in the 1940s, probably in an attempt to draw attention to themselves following the proclamation of the 1936 Land Act. While this Act affirmed the rights to land of most South African groups, it failed to take account of the needs of the Ndebele, presumably because most of them lived as indentured labourers on white farms. Among the Ndzundza Ndebele, therefore, the production of murals can be linked to

a desire to give visible expression to an exclusive ethnic identity. The expression of this identity has become less urgent since South Africa's first democratic election in 1994, when formerly disenfranchised black communities gained the legal right to challenge decisions made on their behalf, but many Ndzundza Ndebele women continue to produce their brightly coloured murals, in part because these wall decorations have become a major tourist attraction.

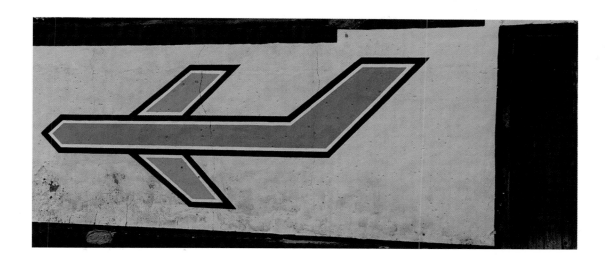

OPPOSITE AND TOP: Some Ndebele wall designs are far less flamboyant than others, consisting of simple black lines painted over a single colour. CENTRE AND ABOVE: The more brightly coloured murals are also characterised by relatively simple designs, often alluding to icons of modern life such as aeroplanes, electric light bulbs and the staircases found in multi-storey buildings.

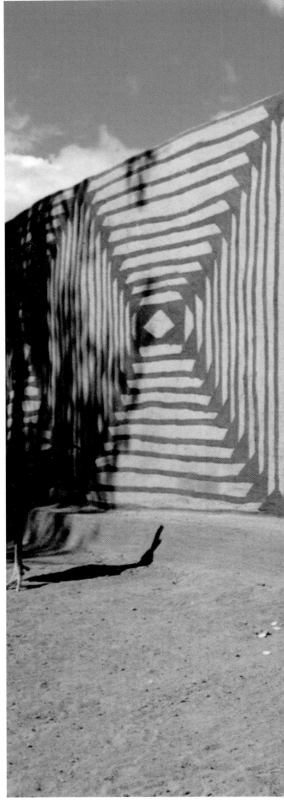

PAGES 156 AND 157: Tsonga murals are unusually large and bold, and can be spotted from far off.
PAGE 158, ABOVE LEFT, AND BELOW LEFT AND RIGHT; AND PAGE 159, TOP LEFT, CENTRE, AND BOTTOM LEFT AND RIGHT: In contrast to Tsonga motifs, those found on South Sotho homes often create unusual optical illusions through the use of stippling paint techniques and the tendency to produce mirror images of starkly painted motifs at regular intervals. Different paint techniques may be combined in the decoration of a single dwelling, and in some cases the doors are incorporated into these designs. PAGE 159, TOP RIGHT: Not all homesteads are necessarily decorated: even among the Venda, and other communities that normally decorate their houses with mural paintings, some women do not do so, either because they lack the time, or through personal aesthetic preferences. Only recently have groups like the Zulu (PAGE 158, TOP RIGHT) and Swazi begun to produce designs of this kind, mainly because their homes traditionally were made entirely from thatched grass.

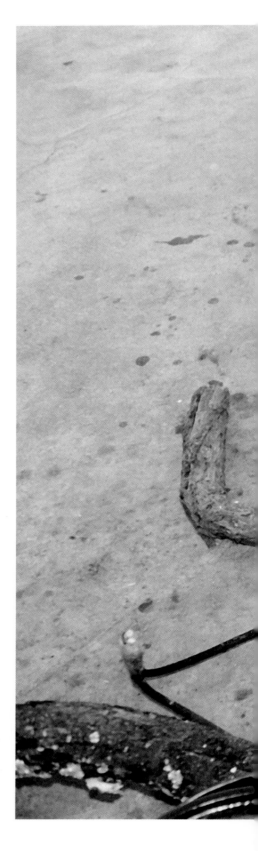

PAGES 160 AND 161: In most rural homes cooking usually takes place in a walled but roofless space that gives sufficient shelter from the wind to allow fires to burn, but also obviates the problem of having to deal with smoke-filled interiors. Zulu and Swazi beehive structures did have hearths, probably because it was easier for smoke to escape from these thatched structures than from homes with mud brick walls.

RIGHT AND PAGES 162 AND 163: Cooking remains the exclusive responsibility of women, but the consumption of meals tends to be communal in all but the most traditional homes, where men still eat separately from women and children.

Many women create bold accents of colour by decorating sections of the interior walls of their homes. This practice, which is common throughout much of South Africa, can be found among groups like the South Sotho (Above) and Ndebele (Opposite, Bottom Left), and has also been adopted among the Venda (Opposite, Centre), by artists like Noria Mabasa (Below). The display of prints, especially of religious images, has increased rapidly in recent years, probably as a sign not only of piety, but also of worldly sophistication.

ABOVE: Although Swazi beehive structures do not lend themselves to decorations of this kind, members of this group string ropes across their dwellings from which they hang cloths and various items of beadwork and other forms of adornment. Unlike people living elsewhere in southern Africa, some Swazi and Zulu traditionalists also continue to sit and sleep on grass mats. BELOW: In contrast to these groups, South Sotho women make clay shelves and sideboards in emulation of the Western practice of displaying plates and other household items in their kitchens and dining-rooms.

index

Page numbers in **bold** refer to a main treatment of a subject; those in *italics* refer to photographs.